Let's Grow Together

A Family's Guide to Health, Fitness, and Emotional Wellness

by
Deidre Wilson

Let's Grow Together

A Family's Guide to Health, Fitness, and Emotional Wellness

Contents

Laying the Foundation for Family Growth

In the heart of every family lies the potential for growth, with every day presenting a new opportunity for deeper connection, understanding, and wellness. The concept of family growth encompasses more than just the individual development of its members; it involves a collective evolution towards stronger emotional bonds, improved communication, and a healthier lifestyle. This book is designed to guide you in nurturing and realizing that potential, transforming the concept into a tangible reality for your family.

The journey towards a healthier, more connected family starts with a solid foundation. Just as a house requires a sturdy base to withstand the pressures of the elements, a family needs a well-laid groundwork to thrive amidst the challenges and stresses of daily life. This foundation is built on several key principles: open communication, mutual respect, shared values, and a commitment to collective and individual health and well-being. By focusing on these areas, families can create an environment that promotes growth, resilience, and happiness.

The pursuit of family growth is a proactive one, requiring both intention and action. It's about making conscious choices towards healthier habits, whether that's in the realm of physical activity, nutrition, mental health, or emotional connection. It's acknowledging that every member of the family has unique needs and contributions, and that addressing these differences enriches the family dynamic rather than detracts from it.

However, laying the foundation for family growth is not without its challenges. In today's fast-paced, technology-driven world, families face myriad pressures, from balancing work and home life to navigating the complex social landscapes that children and adolescents encounter. These pressures can strain even the strongest family bonds. Yet, it is precisely within these challenges that the opportunity for growth lies. By confronting these obstacles together, families can strengthen their resilience, learn valuable life skills, and deepen their connections to one another.

At its core, this book is a guide, designed to empower you with the knowledge, strategies, and inspiration needed to embark on this journey of family growth. It encompasses a broad range of topics, each chosen for its relevance and impact on family health and happiness. From establishing a culture of fitness and mindfulness to navigating difficult conversations and celebrating achievements, the chapters ahead are filled with practical advice, real-world examples, and activities designed to involve every family member.

Understanding the importance of physical and mental health within the family dynamic sets the stage for a lifelong commitment to wellness. Learning how to integrate nutrition and fitness into your family life in a fun and engaging way is not just about forming healthy habits; it's about creating moments of joy and bonding that will be cherished for years to come. Developing mindfulness and stress management techniques offers a pathway to emotional balance and peace, even in the face of life's inevitable challenges. Moreover, establishing routines and rituals can provide a comforting sense of predictability and security, reinforcing family bonds.

The path to family growth is not a linear one; there will be setbacks and challenges along the way. Yet, it is in navigating these moments that some of the most significant growth occurs. Embracing the journey with an open heart and mind will allow you to adapt, learn, and evolve as a family. Remember, growth is not about perfection; it's about progress, resilience, and the deepening of bonds through shared experiences and challenges.

Ultimately, the goal of this book is not just to provide strategies for creating a healthier, happier family but to inspire a shift in perspective. It's about seeing every day as an opportunity to grow closer, to understand each other more deeply, and to build a family life that is rich in love, health, and fulfilment. The foundation you lay today, through the practices and principles shared in these pages, will set the stage for a legacy of family growth that can continue for generations to come.

So let's embark on this journey together, with open minds and willing hearts, ready to embrace the challenges and joys of family growth. With each step forward, you're not just building a healthier family; you're creating a cherished legacy of love, resilience, and wellness that will impact your loved ones for years to come.

Let this book be your guide, a beacon of light on the path to deeper connection, better health, and enduring happiness for your family. Together, we can lay a strong foundation for family growth, transforming challenges into opportunities and dreams into realities.

Chapter 1:
Understanding Family Health

As we step beyond the foundational concepts laid out in the introduction, our journey brings us to the heart of family wellness. Understanding family health isn't just about making sure everyone's fed and getting enough sleep; it's about nurturing a holistic environment where physical, mental, and emotional well-being are in constant, dynamic interplay. Imagine the family as a garden. Just as diverse plants require different care—water, sunlight, and soil nutrients—each family member's health needs are unique yet interconnected. By focusing on the importance of physical health, we begin to see its role in shaping our daily interactions and emotional bonds. Acknowledging this interconnectedness is crucial, as it lays the groundwork for a stronger, more resilient family unit. Amidst the complex, ever-changing rhythms of family life, bridging the gap between mental and emotional wellness becomes our guiding light. This chapter introduces strategies that foster emotional intelligence, ensuring that as we cultivate our physical health, we're also tending to the emotional soil from which our deepest familial connections grow. Through this holistic approach, we embark on a transformative journey towards a unified, thriving family environment.

The Importance of Physical Health in the Family Dynamic

In the intricate tapestry of family life, the weave of physical health holds a place of paramount importance. Its threads, interlaced with emotional and mental well-being, form the fabric that enfolds the family in resilience and vitality. Physical health, often thought of in individual terms, finds its true vibrancy when approached as a collective goal. Its impact on the family dynamic cannot be overstated, as its benefits ripple outward, touching every aspect of familial interaction and bonding.

Consider the scene at any local park: families engaging in physical activities together, whether it's a game of soccer, a brisk walk, or just a playful chase. These moments are not merely about physical fitness; they are the heartbeat of family unity, moments where memories are made and bonds are strengthened. When a family prioritizes physical health, they're setting the stage for shared experiences that are both enriching and nurturing. It's a powerful avenue for teaching life lessons about perseverance, teamwork, and the joy of striving towards a common goal.

Yet, the importance of physical health in the family dynamic extends beyond these visible manifestations. It's a foundation that supports the mental and emotional scaffolding of each family member. Studies have shown that regular physical activity can significantly reduce symptoms of depression and anxiety, and when families engage in these activities together, they amplify these benefits. The shared commitment acts as a buffer against the stresses of life, providing a natural, healthy coping mechanism that draws the family closer.

Furthermore, when parents lead by example, embracing a lifestyle that esteems physical health, they imbue their children with values that last a lifetime. These lessons in discipline, self-care, and healthy living transcend the immediate family unit, preparing the younger generation to embrace these principles in their own lives, and potentially, in the families they may one day have. It's a cyclical gift - one that keeps on giving, cascading through generations, fostering a legacy of health and vigor.

In closing, the significance of physical health within the family dynamic is a beacon that guides the family ship through the tumultuous seas of life. It strengthens the hull, secures the sails, and charts a course towards a horizon filled with vitality, unity, and joy. As families, making the concerted effort to weave physical health into the very fabric of our lives promises not just a fuller, more vibrant present, but a richer, more robust future for all involved. Let us then, move forward with purpose, hand in hand, stride by stride, towards embracing this irreplaceable pillar of family health.

Key Components of Physical Health for All Ages

Understanding the vital aspects of physical health that span across all life stages is crucial for maintaining a well-rounded, vibrant family lifestyle. When we talk about physical health, it's not simply about the absence of illness, but rather a state of complete physical well-being. This encompasses regular physical activity, a balanced diet, adequate rest, and preventive healthcare measures. Our goal is to equip each family member with the knowledge and habits that foster lifelong health and vitality, understanding that these components evolve with age but their importance remains constant.

Regular physical activity is the cornerstone of good health for individuals at any age. It strengthens muscles, improves cardiovascular health, enhances flexibility, and boosts mental health. It's essential to tailor activities to be age-appropriate, ensuring that they are engaging and fun for children, yet challenging and fulfilling for adults. The aim is to integrate physical activity into daily routines, making it a natural and enjoyable part of family life. Whether it's a family hike, a dance-off in the living room, or a yoga session together, what's important is moving and creating those healthy patterns from the youngest to the eldest in the household.

Another critical component is nutrition. A balanced diet provides the energy and nutrients necessary for growth, repair, and overall well-being. Making nutrition a family affair not only educates children about healthy eating from a young age but also encourages adults to make healthier choices. Involving the whole family in meal planning and preparation can make this venture more enjoyable and impactful. Adequate rest, too, cannot be overstated. Sleep plays a critical role in physical and mental health, affecting mood, energy levels, and even the immune system. Emphasizing the importance of a good night's sleep for everyone strengthens the foundation of a healthy, happy family. Lastly, regular check-ups and preventive healthcare measures contribute significantly to identifying and addressing potential health issues early. Together, these elements form a mosaic of practices that nourish the body and cultivate a life of vitality and joy for all family members.

Bridging Mental and Emotional Wellness

In today's fast-paced world, where the lines between work and home often blur, ensuring mental and emotional wellness within the family structure has never been more critical. Each family member brings their own set of experiences and emotions to the table, making understanding and empathy key to a healthy family dynamic. It's easy to focus on physical health as it's often more visible, but the mind and emotions play an equally vital role in overall well-being.

Mental and emotional wellness involves recognizing emotions, understanding how and why they occur, and handling them in a healthy way. This doesn't mean being happy all the time; rather, it's about balance and resilience. Teaching our children to identify their feelings, express them appropriately, and manage stress positively are essential skills. This not only nurtures their mental health but also sets a foundation for their emotional intelligence, crucial for all aspects of life.

The synergy between mental and emotional wellness and family health is undeniable. When one member struggles, it affects the entire family. Hence, creating a supportive environment where each person feels heard and valued is paramount. Regular family meetings can be a great forum for expressing concerns and emotions in a safe space. These meetings, coupled with individual check-ins, ensure that no one feels isolated with their struggles.

Moreover, fostering a positive home environment that encourages open communication and mutual respect is crucial. Celebrate each other's successes and be there during failures, offering a shoulder to lean on. Activities that promote mental and emotional well-being, such as mindfulness exercises, family meditation, or simply spending quality time together, can strengthen bonds. Remember, it's not about having a perfect family but about being a united one amidst the ups and downs.

As we navigate through the chapters of our lives, let's remind ourselves that bridging mental and emotional wellness within the family is an ongoing journey. It requires patience, effort, and a lot of love. By embedding these practices into the fabric of our family life, we pave the way for a healthier, happier tomorrow. Together, we can create a strong support system, where challenges are met with understanding and grace, leading to a thriving family environment that nurtures growth in every sense.

Strategies for Fostering Emotional Intelligence

In today's fast-paced world, the ability to navigate one's emotions and the emotions of others plays a crucial role not just in individual well-being but in the health and cohesion of families too. Fostering emotional intelligence within the family environment is akin to nurturing a garden. It requires patience, understanding, and consistent care. The emphasis here is on strategies that parents can employ to cultivate a household where everyone can recognize, understand, manage, and communicate their feelings in constructive ways.

Understanding and validating each other's emotions is the cornerstone of developing emotional intelligence. When family members feel heard and understood, it creates a safe space for open communication. Encourage daily check-ins where each person shares something about their day along with how it made them feel. This simple practice teaches children and adults alike to associate their experiences with emotional responses, promoting a deeper self-awareness and empathy towards others. Additionally, it's essential to model appropriate emotional reactions. Children, especially, learn from observing adults. Showing them how to deal with disappointment, anger, or excitement in healthy ways sets a strong foundation for their emotional development.

Conflict resolution plays a significant role in enhancing emotional intelligence. Instead of shying away from disagreements, use them as opportunities to teach problem-solving skills. Guide your family through identifying the problem, expressing their feelings without blame, brainstorming solutions together, and deciding on a course of action that respects everyone's emotions. This not only helps in resolving the current issue but equips children and adults with the tools to handle future conflicts more adeptly. By integrating these strategies into your family life, you're not only addressing the emotional needs of the present but are laying down the groundwork for a future where your family navigates life's ups and downs with emotional savvy and resilience.

Chapter 2:
Nutrition as a Family Affair

Embarking on the journey of nutritional wellness within the sphere of the family can be both a challenging and profoundly rewarding expedition. Nutrition isn't just a personal affair; it's a collective endeavor that holds the power to bind a family closer, guiding each member towards a healthier, more vibrant life. It's about more than just eating the right foods; it's about fostering an environment where making healthier choices becomes a seamless, even enjoyable part of daily life. Imagine transforming meal planning from a task into an engaging activity that involves each family member, blending educational moments with fun, interactive sessions. This chapter aims to show you how to make nutrition a cornerstone of family activity, how to creatively plan balanced meals together, and integrate nutrition education into your everyday conversations without it feeling like a chore. It will also address the unique challenges that inevitably arise, such as dealing with picky eaters or dietary restrictions, with practical, compassionate strategies for overcoming these hurdles together. By embracing nutrition as a family affair, you're setting the stage for lifelong habits that will support the physical and emotional well-being of every member of your family. Let's transform mealtime into a journey of discovery, a time for growth, and a celebration of mutual support and love.

Planning Balanced Meals Together

In the journey toward a healthier family life, meal planning emerges as a pivotal ritual that can transform mundane meal prepping into a dynamic familial bonding activity. It's much more than deciding what's for dinner; it's about nurturing habits, knowledge, and a sense of responsibility in your children while ensuring everyone's nutritional needs are met. The act of planning balanced meals together does wonders in demystifying the complexities of nutrition and turning it into a hands-on, collaborative effort.

Imagine the kitchen transforming into a lively hub of learning and laughter where each family member gets to voice their preferences and learn about the nutrients their body needs. This doesn't mean that meals need to be perfectly balanced at every sitting, but rather that over time, meals collectively cater to the nutritional needs of the family. It's important to recognize and celebrate the diversity in tastes and nutritional requirements within your family. This inclusive approach not only accommodates picky eaters but also sparks curiosity about different food groups and how they contribute to our well-being.

Integrating nutrition education doesn't have to be a formal affair. Casual conversations about why we choose certain ingredients over others or the benefits of staying hydrated can be immensely educational. When children understand the 'why' behind the food choices you're encouraging, they're more likely to embrace those choices themselves. To facilitate this, consider designating a day where each family member can pick a meal based on a specific nutrient or food group. This activity can become a fun, educational challenge that everyone looks forward to, encouraging both teamwork and individual research.

Addressing dietary challenges and picky eating habits becomes substantially easier when meals are planned together. When children feel they have a say in what's on their plate, resistance tends to wane. It also presents an opportunity to discuss the nutritional value of different foods, encouraging a more open-minded approach to eating. However, the aim is not to force changes but to welcome them gently, through understanding and patience. It's not just about the food on the table but about encouraging a proactive, informed attitude towards nutrition and health.

Inculcating these habits and attitudes towards meal planning and balanced eating may not yield overnight success, but it's a step towards fostering a healthy relationship with food in your children. This collaborative process reinforces the idea that taking care of one's health is not only a personal responsibility but also a shared family value. Through planning and enjoying meals together, your family can grow closer, healthier, and more knowledgeable about the nutrients that fuel their bodies and minds.

Integrating Nutrition Education in Everyday Conversations is about seamlessly weaving the threads of nutritional wisdom into the fabric of our daily family interactions. It's about transforming mealtime chats, grocery shopping trips, and even snack time into opportunities for learning and growth. Imagine engaging your child in a conversation about the vibrant colors on their plate and what these colors mean for their body - not just at the dinner table but during a leisurely walk or while drawing together. This is not about formal lectures but about nurturing curiosity and understanding through casual, meaningful dialogue.

It's easy to overlook the power of a spontaneous conversation about food choices when we're bombarded with messages about diet culture and quick fixes. Yet, these everyday moments hold immense potential for teaching children how to connect with their food and listen to their bodies. By discussing how different foods can affect their energy levels and mood, we not only educate them but also empower them to make healthier choices. This approach encourages children to view food as a source of nourishment and pleasure, fostering a positive relationship with eating that can last a lifetime.

Moreover, integrating nutrition education into everyday conversations paves the way for a family culture that values well-being and informed choices. It's about creating an environment where children feel comfortable asking questions, exploring new foods, and expressing their preferences. This dialogue can also extend beyond the immediate family, including friends and relatives, thus spreading the seeds of nutritional wisdom through communities. By embracing nutrition education as a natural part of daily life, we open the door to a healthier, more conscious future for our families. Let's make every conversation an opportunity to build a foundation of knowledge, respect, and appreciation for the food that fuels our lives.

Addressing Picky Eaters and Dietary Challenges

Navigating the stormy seas of picky eaters and dietary restrictions can often feel like a daunting task for any parent. But let's shift our perspective for a moment. These challenges aren't roadblocks; they're opportunities to embrace creativity, understanding, and patience in our family's nutritional journey. It's essential to remember that a person's relationship with food is deeply personal and evolves over time. By approaching this with empathy and open-mindedness, we create an environment where every family member feels supported and heard.

When dealing with a picky eater, the first step is to involve them in the food selection and preparation process. This approach isn't just about giving them a choice; it's about empowering them with knowledge and ownership over what they eat. Visit farmers markets or grocery stores together and engage in discussions about different foods, their origins, and benefits. Cooking together can transform mealtime from a battleground to a shared adventure, making new or previously rejected foods more intriguing and appealing.

Understanding the root cause of picky eating or dietary constraints is also crucial. Is it a texture issue? A flavor dislike? Or perhaps a dietary sensitivity? By pinpointing the specifics, you can tailor meals that respect these preferences while still pushing the envelope ever so gently. For example, if texture is an issue, introducing smoothies or creatively blended soups could be a hit. The goal is gradual exposure, gradually expanding the eater's comfort zone without making them feel pressured or overwhelmed.

It's also beneficial to create a mealtime atmosphere that prioritizes connection and enjoyment over consumption. This means engaging in meaningful conversations, sharing stories, and fostering a relaxed environment. Pressure, bribery, or negative comments about eating habits can exacerbate picky eating behaviors and create negative associations with food. Instead, emphasize the positive aspects of mealtime, celebrating even the small victories, like trying a tiny piece of a new vegetable or agreeing to have it on their plate.

Lastly, patience and consistency are your best allies. Changing dietary habits and expanding palates won't happen overnight. It is a gradual process that requires understanding, encouragement, and occasionally, a bit of creativity. Celebrate progress, no matter how small, and remain flexible. Some strategies might work wonders one week and fall flat the next, and that's perfectly okay. By fostering a family culture that values nutritional health, shared experiences, and mutual respect, navigating picky eating and dietary challenges can become less of a hurdle and more of a journey of growth for both parents and children.

Chapter 3:
Fitness Fun for the Whole Family

In the journey to foster a holistic and thriving family environment, integrating fitness into your daily routine emerges as a powerful tool not just for individual health, but for strengthening the family bond as well. Imagine transforming the often solitary endeavor of exercise into a source of joy, laughter, and connection for everyone in the family. This chapter delves into practical strategies for making physical activity a pillar of family life, regardless of age or fitness level. It's about shaking off the notion of exercise as a chore and embracing it as an opportunity for creating lasting memories together. From spontaneous dance-offs in the living room to nature hikes that double as treasure hunts, we'll explore diverse and accessible ways to keep everyone engaged and excited about moving their bodies. The secret lies in customizing activities to fit the unique needs and interests of each family member, turning workouts into playouts, and setting a foundation of healthy habits that children will carry into adulthood. By prioritizing fun and inclusivity, you'll discover not only a path to better physical health but also an enriching strategy for nurturing closer relationships and crafting a vibrant family culture that celebrates being active together.

Creating an Active Lifestyle for Everyone

Moving into a lifestyle that embraces activity and fitness as a core value may seem daunting, especially with the differing needs and interests of each family member. However, the transformation towards a more active lifestyle is not only essential for physical health but serves as a vibrant foundation for mental and emotional well-being. It's about creating moments together that are lively, fun, and enriching, forging stronger family bonds through shared experiences.

Initiating this change can start small - it doesn't have to be a drastic overhaul. Simple activities like evening walks, bike rides, or even gardening together can kickstart this new chapter. Each of these activities offers not just physical benefits but also opportunities for conversation, sharing, and connection. The key is consistency and inclusion, ensuring that everyone, regardless of age or ability, has a role to play in this active lifestyle. This approach demystifies fitness, making it accessible and enjoyable for all.

Customization is crucial. Recognize and celebrate the uniqueness of each family member by introducing activities that cater to different interests and abilities. From dance-offs in the living room to family yoga sessions or obstacle courses in the backyard, variety keeps engagement high and complacency at bay. Moreover, involving everyone in the planning process empowers each member, giving them a voice and a sense of ownership over their health and happiness.

Beyond physical activities, anchoring this lifestyle in the routines of your daily life embeds a sense of normalcy and importance to staying active. Whether it's opting to take the stairs instead of the elevator, parking a bit farther from the grocery store entrance, or having impromptu dance breaks while doing household chores, these small choices add up, making a significant impact over time. It's about weaving movement and activity into the fabric of your family life so that it becomes second nature.

Finally, celebrate progress, no matter how small. Setting achievable goals and recognizing when they're met fosters a culture of positivity and encouragement. It's not just about the end results—acknowledge the effort, resilience, and teamwork it takes to get there. This not only motivates but also strengthens the family unit. Remember, creating an active lifestyle for everyone is a journey, one that promises to be filled with growth, joy, and countless memories for your family. Let's embrace it with open arms, one step at a time.

Customizing Family Fitness to Each Member's Needs

Embarking on a fitness journey as a family doesn't mean adopting a one-size-fits-all approach. It's about recognizing and respecting each member's unique needs, abilities, and interests, ensuring that family fitness is not just a collective effort but a personal journey for everyone involved. Every family member, from toddlers to grandparents, has differing physical capabilities and preferences. It's vital to approach family fitness with flexibility, understanding that customizing activities to suit each individual can significantly enhance engagement and long-term commitment to an active lifestyle.

When planning fitness activities, consider the individual goals and limitations of family members. For adolescents seeking to boost their sports performance, incorporating specific strength and agility exercises might be beneficial, whereas older family members might prefer low-impact activities such as walking, swimming, or yoga. For younger children, games that promote movement, such as tag or playful obstacle courses, can make physical activity fun and engaging. By including a variety of activities, you ensure that everyone finds something they enjoy, fostering a positive association with exercise. It's about finding a balance between pushing each other to improve while acknowledging and celebrating the differing stages of everyone's fitness journey.

Moreover, involving each family member in the planning process can be immensely empowering. It's an opportunity for everyone to voice their preferences, interests, and concerns, thereby making collective decisions that honor individual needs. Such inclusivity not only strengthens family bonds but also ensures that the devised fitness plan is realistic, achievable, and enjoyable for all. This tailored approach makes the pursuit of health and wellness an exciting adventure that everyone looks forward to, transforming it from a mundane task into a cherished part of family life. Ultimately, by customizing family fitness to each member's needs, you nurture a culture of health that is adaptable, inclusive, and sustainable, laying the foundation for lifelong well-being and togetherness.

The Role of Play and Outdoor Activities

In the bustling rhythm of daily life, taking a moment to pause and embrace the simplicity of play and the vastness of outdoor activities can seem like a luxury we can scarcely afford. However, it's exactly this mindset that we need to shift. The role of play and engagement with the outdoors isn't just an additional part of our lives; it's a fundamental aspect of fostering a healthy, vibrant family dynamic. It's about more than just the physical benefits; it's a vital component for mental and emotional well-being too. Let's delve into why incorporating these elements into our family life isn't just important but essential.

First and foremost, play and outdoor activities provide an unparalleled opportunity for physical exercise. In an era where screens often dominate our leisure time, being active outside encourages everyone in the family to move more, improving cardiovascular health, flexibility, and strength. But it's not just about the physical aspect; it's about the joy, laughter, and connections that come from shared experiences. Whether it's a game of tag in the backyard, a family hike, or an impromptu soccer match, these moments are where memories are made, bonds are strengthened, and a sense of belonging is reinforced.

Beyond the physical and emotional connections, play and outdoor activities are incredibly versatile in teaching valuable life skills. These settings offer natural opportunities for children and adults alike to learn about teamwork, leadership, problem-solving, and persistence. Overcoming a challenging hike, learning to ride a bike, or even setting up a tent all offer lessons in overcoming obstacles, setting and achieving goals, and working together. It's in these unstructured, spontaneous moments that some of the most impactful lessons are learned.

Fostering an appreciation for nature is another invaluable byproduct of spending time outdoors. In today's world, understanding and respecting our environment is more important than ever. Through outdoor activities, families can cultivate a sense of responsibility and care for the world around them. Experiencing the beauty and complexity of nature firsthand can inspire a lifetime of environmental stewardship and a deeper connection to the planet that supports us all.

Embarking on the journey of incorporating play and outdoor activities into our family lives requires intention and creativity, but the benefits far outweigh the effort. It's about breaking the cycle of sedentary lifestyles and creating a culture within our families that values and prioritizes health, joy, and togetherness. The memories we make, the lessons we learn, and the connections we forge through these shared experiences are the threads that weave the fabric of a strong, healthy, and unified family. So, let's step outside, let's play, and let's grow together as families in both body and spirit.

Chapter 4:
Mindfulness and Stress Management Techniques

In the whirlwind of day-to-day life, stress can often go unnoticed until it manifests in more concerning ways, affecting both our personal well-being and our family dynamics. Understanding this, it becomes paramount to incorporate mindfulness and stress management techniques into our daily routines to foster a harmonious home environment. This chapter dives into practical strategies that are designed to cultivate a mindfulness practice that resonates with both children and adults, ensuring that every family member can find solace and strength within their own minds. By exploring activities that range from simple breathing exercises to more structured mindfulness practices, we're given the tools to not only confront our stress but to transform our reaction to it, creating a domino effect of positivity within the family unit. Furthermore, by managing stress collectively, we lay down a foundation of support, empathy, and understanding, reinforcing the idea that no one is alone in their journey. The power of shared experiences in stress management cannot be understated; it strengthens familial bonds and teaches invaluable lessons in compassion and resilience. Let's embark on this journey of mindfulness together, embracing each moment as an opportunity for growth, connection, and deepened understanding, transforming our collective family stress into a source of collective family strength.

Cultivating a Practice of Mindfulness in the Family

Introducing mindfulness into your family's routine might seem like a tall order amidst the hustle and bustle of everyday life. Yet, the benefits of creating a mindful environment at home can be profound, fostering deeper connections, reducing stress, and setting a foundation of emotional intelligence that supports healthy development. It begins with a simple commitment to be more present, both with ourselves and with each other, navigating the complexities of modern life with a sense of calm and understanding. It's about embracing the moment, guiding our families to live less in the noise of what's next and more in the beauty of now.

Mindfulness doesn't have to be a daunting task. It can be as simple as starting a tradition of sharing daily gratitude around the dinner table or introducing a quiet time where each family member can explore individual contemplative practices like reading, drawing, or even meditating. The idea is to create pockets of peace within your daily routine that invite stillness and reflection. This could be a moment of deep breathing together before starting the day or an evening walk where the focus is on observing the natural world around you. It's these small, yet consistent practices that weave mindfulness into the fabric of family life.

One of the most compelling reasons to cultivate mindfulness within the family is its ability to enhance emotional resilience. By learning to be mindful, we teach our children how to handle life's ups and downs with grace. Mindfulness equips them with the tools to observe their emotions without judgment, understand their transient nature, and respond rather than react to situations. This skill, developed in the warmth of a supportive family environment, becomes a cornerstone of their emotional health as they grow.

Developing a family mindfulness practice also opens up avenues for richer communication. It encourages an atmosphere where feelings are acknowledged and personal experiences are valued. Imagine a family discussion where everyone feels heard and respected, or where conflicts are resolved through mutual understanding rather than heated arguments. Such is the potential when mindfulness informs our interactions; it cultivates a heart-centered approach to communication that strengthens the bond between family members.

Embarking on this journey towards a more mindful family life invites a world of growth and discovery for everyone involved. It's an opportunity to lay the groundwork for lifelong values of compassion, self-awareness, and emotional balance. The path may require patience and practice, but the rewards—a family life rich in connection, understanding, and peace—are inestimable. Begin with small steps, celebrate the victories along the way, and watch as the seeds of mindfulness you plant today flourish into a vibrant, healthy family dynamic.

Mindfulness Activities Suitable for Children and Adults

In today's fast-paced world, the importance of slowing down and being present in the moment cannot be overstated, especially when it comes to nurturing a healthy family dynamic. Mindfulness, the practice of paying attention to the present moment with openness, curiosity, and without judgment, is a powerful tool that both children and adults can benefit from. It's about noticing what's happening inside and outside of ourselves moment by moment and can significantly enhance our mental and emotional well-being.

Starting with something as simple as mindful breathing can lay the foundation for a more attentive and connected family life. This exercise involves focusing solely on the breath, noticing the sensation of air entering and exiting the body, which can help calm the mind and reduce stress. For children, this can be introduced as a "breathing buddy" practice where they lie down with a stuffed animal on their stomachs, watching it rise and fall as they breathe. This not only makes the activity engaging for them but also teaches them to be aware of their breath in a fun and relatable way. For adults, extending mindful breathing to a few minutes of quiet, focused attention each day can provide a much-needed pause from the hustle and bustle of daily life.

Another activity that families can enjoy together is the "mindful walk," which involves taking a leisurely walk and paying close attention to the sights, sounds, smells, and sensations experienced. It's a wonderful way to connect with nature and each other, encouraging conversations about what each family member notices and feels during the walk. This exercise teaches us to be aware of our surroundings and find joy and wonder in the little things, strengthening our bond with the world around us and with each other. By integrating these mindfulness practices into daily routines, families can cultivate a more conscious, present, and harmonious lifestyle, laying a strong foundation for mental and emotional health that benefits everyone in the family.

Techniques for Managing Stress Together

Living in a world that is ever-changing and often challenging, families face their share of stressors. However, stress doesn't have to be a divisive element within the family unit. Instead, embracing stress management techniques together can strengthen bonds, improve mental health, and foster a nurturing environment where everyone feels supported. It's essential to approach stress management as a team, crafting a safe space where each member feels valued and heard.

Firstly, establishing a regular family mindfulness practice can be incredibly beneficial. This could range from shared meditation sessions to simply spending a few moments in silence together before starting your day. Such activities don't necessitate a lot of time; rather, it's the consistency and collective participation that counts. The idea here is to cultivate an atmosphere of calm and focused presence, making it easier to tackle the day's challenges with a sense of collective composure.

Open communication is also vital in managing stress as a family. Encourage discussions about feelings and stressors in a non-judgmental setting. This practice helps in identifying what each family member is going through and offers opportunities to support each other. For instance, holding a weekly "family meeting" where everyone has the floor to express themselves can make a huge difference. It reinforces the idea that while individual experiences may differ, the family faces challenges together.

Incorporating physical activities into your family's routine is another effective stress management strategy. Exercise is well-documented for its stress-relieving benefits, and doing it together amplifies the positive effects. Whether it's a weekend hike, a nightly dance party in the living room, or a morning yoga session, find activities that get everyone moving and laughing together. It's about making joy and health integral parts of your family's daily life.

Lastly, remember to celebrate and acknowledge the efforts each family member makes towards managing and coping with stress. Recognizing even the small victories instills a sense of achievement and supports a resilient mindset. As you navigate stress as a family, know that the journey is as much about building enduring connections as it is about overcoming challenges. By focusing on empathy, support, and open communication, you're not just managing stress—you're transforming it into an opportunity for growth and togetherness.

Chapter 5:
The Power of Routine and Structure

Embarking on the journey of instilling structure and routine into your family's life can be transformational. At its core, a well-crafted routine is not about rigid schedules or stifling spontaneity; it's about creating a framework that empowers each family member to thrive. When we introduce regular schedules for meals, fitness, and quality time together, we're not just organizing our days; we're reinforcing the importance of health, well-being, and connection within our family unit. An effective routine serves as a safety net, providing comfort and predictability in a world that's often unpredictable. It's about balancing the hustle of daily life with moments that reconnect us, whether that's a nightly dinner or a weekend nature hike. As you weave these threads of routine and structure through the fabric of your family life, you'll notice a remarkable shift. Stress levels often decrease because everyone knows what to expect and when to expect it. This clarity fosters independence in children as they take on age-appropriate responsibilities within the family's routine. Moreover, carving out dedicated time for collective activities strengthens family bonds, making it easier to navigate the ups and downs of life together. In this chapter, we'll explore how to establish routines that resonate with your family's unique rhythm, ensuring there's always room for flexibility and growth. Remember, the strongest structures are those that can bend without breaking, and it's this balance that will help your family not just survive but thrive.

Establishing Effective Family Routines

Imagine a world where every member of the family operates in harmonious sync, understanding not only their responsibilities but also embracing the collective journey toward health, happiness, and growth. This isn't a far-fetched fantasy—it's an attainable reality through the power of effective family routines. Establishing a structure that supports every family member's needs, while also allowing room for flexibility, is essential in fostering an environment where each person can thrive.

Routines offer a backbone of predictability in the whirlwind of life. For children especially, a consistent routine provides a sense of security and stability, allowing them to develop confidence and independence. For adults, it can alleviate the stress of daily decision-making, freeing up mental energy for more creative and fulfilling pursuits. But how do we strike the right balance? It begins with communication, understanding each person's needs, preferences, and obligations, and weaving them into a cohesive plan that aligns with the family's overarching goals.

Start with the basics: mealtimes, bedtime routines, and family activities. Regularly scheduled meals can become more than just eating times—they're opportunities for nourishment, learning, and bonding. A consistent bedtime routine aids not just in better sleep but also in creating a calm, reflective end to the day. Weekly family activities, be it a game night or a neighborhood walk, reinforce the sense of unity and belonging. These are the pillars upon which additional routines can be built, tailored to your family's unique dynamic.

Flexibility within this structure is crucial. Life is unpredictable, and the ability to adapt without losing sight of your family's routines is a valuable skill. Treat the unexpected as teachable moments, showing your children how to pivot gracefully in the face of change. This balancing act of routine and flexibility teaches resilience, a quality that will serve them well throughout life. Remember, it's not about adhering rigidly to a schedule; it's about the rhythm and flow that best supports your family's well-being.

As we delve deeper into the importance of routines, let's keep in mind that the ultimate goal is to cultivate a family life filled with joy, growth, and mutual support. Establishing effective family routines isn't just about organization—it's about creating a framework that allows every member to flourish both individually and collectively. With dedication, patience, and love, you can build a foundation that empowers your family to navigate life's challenges and celebrate its joys together.

The Balancing Act: Flexibility Within Structure is akin to finding the right rhythm in a dance between consistency and adaptability. Imagine you're setting the stage for your family's daily life with a framework that's both sturdy and yet, can sway gently to the rhythm of life's unforeseeable twists and turns. It's about crafting a schedule that accommodate the needs, the surprises, and the growth of each family member. This isn't about rigidity. Far from it. This is about creating a cocoon of stability, within which every individual can flutter and thrive, adapting to change without breaking stride.

In the heart of nurturing a family, embracing the concept of flexibility within a structured environment means recognizing when to hold firm and when to let go. It's understanding that while routines are immensely beneficial in providing a sense of security and order, they shouldn't become chains that bind us too tightly. For instance, perhaps your family thrives on having dinner together every night—a wonderful routine that fosters connection and communication. However, if an unexpected opportunity arises for your child to engage in a spontaneous playdate or a last-minute family event crops up, it's okay to adjust. The core value isn't in the act of dining together, but in ensuring that your family is finding meaningful ways to connect, whether that's at the dinner table or through shared experiences.

Finally, remember that integrating flexibility within structure is an ongoing process that requires patience, communication, and a bit of creativity. It's about sitting down with your family, discussing what's working and what's not, and being open to tweaking routines as your family evolves. Perhaps most importantly, it's about showing your children, through your actions and decisions, that adaptability is not just a strategy for managing a family schedule but an invaluable life skill. By mastering this balancing act, you're not just organizing time; you're teaching your children how to navigate life's ebb and flow with grace, resilience, and a positive spirit.

Rituals that Strengthen Family Bonds

In the heart of every family's success lies the rituals that bind them, offering a unique blend of strength and comfort amidst life's chaos. These rituals, often simple in practice, possess the profound ability to knit the fabric of family bonds tighter, fostering a sense of belonging and identity among its members. As we delve into the Power of Routine and Structure, it's essential to recognize how rituals, those repeated actions imbued with meaning, play a pivotal role in strengthening the family unit.

Rituals come in various forms, from daily habits to seasonal traditions, each carrying its own weight in building resilience and unity. Consider the power of a family meal; this daily gathering is not just about nourishment but becomes a sacred time for connection, sharing, and listening. It's a moment paused from the day's hustle, dedicated entirely to being present with one another. Encouraging open dialogue and active listening during these times enhances mutual respect and understanding, creating a foundation strong enough to support each family member's growth and well-being.

Seasonal rituals, whether it's holiday traditions, annual vacations, or celebrating milestones, also play a crucial role. These events offer a framework for creating lasting memories and reinforcing family values, providing a sense of continuity and security. Embracing these shared experiences encourages each family member to contribute, fostering a culture of inclusivity and appreciation for one another's uniqueness. This collective involvement not only enhances the ritual's meaningfulness but also reinforces the family's interconnectedness.

Integrating mindfulness and gratitude into daily rituals can elevate their impact on family bonds. Starting or ending the day with a gratitude circle, where each person shares something they're thankful for, shifts the focus to the positives, promoting a healthy perspective on life's challenges. This practice cultivates an environment of positivity and support, where family members feel valued and heard. It's a gentle reminder of the strength derived from unity and the importance of cherishing each moment together.

The power of rituals extends beyond the actions themselves; it lies in their ability to evolve with the family, adapting to changes and growing needs. As families embark on this journey of creating and maintaining rituals, they pave the way for a legacy of love, resilience, and unity. So, embrace the beauty of rituals, for in these repeated, meaningful actions, families find their strength, identity, and the boundless power of their bonds.

Chapter 6:
Navigating Difficult Conversations and Emotional Health

As families journey through life together, they inevitably encounter moments that test their emotional resilience and communication skills. These moments, from minor disagreements to major crises, require a nuanced approach to ensure the emotional health of each family member is not only preserved but also nurtured. Navigating difficult conversations requires more than just patience; it demands strategy, empathy, and a commitment to mutual understanding. With the right techniques, families can transform challenging dialogues into opportunities for growth and deeper connection. This chapter aims to equip you with tools and strategies for effective family communication, offering support mechanisms that stand firm in the face of conflict and change. Together, we'll explore how to build a resilient family unit capable of withstanding the pressures of life while maintaining a framework of support, understanding, and love. By fostering an environment where emotions are respected and voices heard, every member can develop the coping skills needed to navigate the complexities of life, turning potential obstacles into stepping stones toward a healthier, more emotionally connected family dynamic.

Strategies for Effective Communication within the Family

In every family's journey toward a healthier, more connected life, the cornerstone lies in mastering the art of communication. It's not just about talking more; it's about creating an environment where every voice, big or small, feels heard and valued. Imagine the family as a garden, where each member is a unique plant that needs the right amount of sunlight, water, and soil to thrive. Just as plants communicate their needs through their leaves and flowers, family members express their needs through words and actions. It's crucial for family members to actively listen to each other, not just wait for their turn to speak. Active listening involves hearing the spoken words, understanding the emotions behind them, and responding in a way that makes the speaker feel heard and valued.

Setting aside specific times for family meetings can be a game-changer in enhancing communication. However, these meetings shouldn't be approached with dread, like a corporate boardroom gathering. Instead, think of them as a safe space where everyone, from the youngest to the oldest, can share their thoughts, feelings, and needs openly and without judgment. During these meetings, discuss everything from daily schedules and responsibilities to hopes, worries, and dreams. It can be beneficial to establish some ground rules, such as one person speaking at a time and avoiding interruptions, to ensure that communication is respectful and productive.

Moreover, in the digital age, where screens often replace human interaction, it's vital to encourage face-to-face conversations. While technology can be a tool for staying connected, nothing can substitute the warmth and authenticity of talking in person. Family meals, for instance, provide a perfect opportunity for everyone to share their day's experiences, laugh together, and strengthen their bonds. It's during these unguarded moments that families can truly connect and understand each other on a deeper level.

Conflict is a natural part of any relationship, and how it's handled can either strengthen or weaken family ties. When disagreements arise, it's important to address them calmly and constructively, ensuring that everyone's feelings and viewpoints are considered. Instead of assigning blame, focus on finding solutions together. This approach not only resolves the issue at hand but also teaches valuable life skills of negotiation, empathy, and problem-solving. Remember, the goal is not to win the argument but to maintain harmony and understanding within the family.

Lastly, consider the power of appreciation and positive reinforcement. Recognizing and expressing gratitude for each other's efforts and achievements, no matter how small, can significantly boost morale and self-esteem. A simple "thank you" or "I'm proud of you" can go a long way in reinforcing positive behavior and encouraging open, honest, and loving communication. As you navigate the complexities of family life, remember that effective communication is the key to nurturing a healthy, happy, and resilient family unit. Together, you can overcome any challenge and celebrate every triumph as a strong, unified team.

Support Mechanisms for Times of Family Strife

In every family's journey, there will be times of turmoil and discomfort. It's during these moments that the strength of our bonds is truly tested, underscoring the necessity for robust support mechanisms. These tools aren't just about weathering the storm but also about emerging stronger and more united than before.

First and foremost, open communication stands as the bedrock of any solid family unit. Encouraging each member to express their thoughts and feelings without fear of judgment fosters an atmosphere of mutual respect and understanding. Remember, it's not just about talking; it's equally about listening. Active listening helps in recognizing the emotions behind the words, allowing for a compassionate response. By institutionalizing this practice, your family can develop a reflexive habit of turning towards each other, rather than away, in times of strife.

Beyond the home, seeking external support can be invaluable. This may take the form of family therapy or counseling, where a neutral third party can facilitate deeper conversations and provide professional guidance. In the current digital age, there are also countless online resources and support groups that cater to specific challenges facing families. These platforms can offer fresh perspectives and strategies that perhaps hadn't been considered. Additionally, engaging in community activities can serve as a respite and source of strength. Whether it's a sports team, a religious group, or a hobby club, such gatherings reinforce the sense that your family is not alone in its struggles.

Lastly, never underestimate the power of shared experiences in healing and bonding. Whether it's a daily ritual, like sharing a meal, or a special activity, such as a weekend getaway, these moments can serve as anchors, reminding each family member of the love and joy that exists amongst you. These are the building blocks of resilience, enabling your family to not only survive but thrive through times of strife.

Building Resilience and Coping Skills Together

In the journey of family life, confrontations and emotional upheavals are as inevitable as the changing seasons. Yet, it's not these challenges themselves but how we navigate them that truly defines the strength and health of our family unit. Building resilience and developing coping skills together is vital, providing each member with the armor needed to face life's battles head-on. Resilience isn't innate; it's crafted through persistent effort, mutual support, and a shared commitment to growth.

Imagine resilience as a muscle. Just like physical strength, it requires training, nourishment, and recovery. Families can "train" their resilience muscle through open communication, validating each member's feelings, and collectively finding solutions to problems. It's about creating a safe space where emotions are not just acknowledged but are seen as a dashboard indicating what needs attention within the family dynamics. When facing difficulties, remember that resilience is also about knowing when to ease the pressure and give time for recovery, ensuring that the family unit remains a source of comfort and security for all.

Coping skills are the tools in our resilience toolkit. They can range from simple breathing exercises during times of stress to structured family meetings to address more significant issues. Encouraging activities like mindfulness, shared hobbies, or regular physical exercise can greatly enhance a family's collective coping strategies. These mechanisms don't just help manage existing stress; they preemptively strengthen the family's ability to deal with future challenges. It's crucial that these skills are practiced regularly, not just pulled out in times of crisis, to be most effective.

Building these skills is a collaborative effort that requires everyone's participation. It's about leaning on each other and recognizing that vulnerability is not a weakness but a courageous step towards genuine connection and understanding. When one member struggles, the family can rally, providing not just a buffer against the hardship but a scaffold encouraging growth beyond it. This collaborative resilience- building fosters a sense of unity, belonging, and understanding that fortifies the family against any challenge.

The beauty of this process is in its reciprocal nature. As you invest in building resilience and coping skills within your family, each member becomes a beacon of support, not just within the household but in their interactions outside of it. You are, in essence, contributing to a healthier, more resilient community. The resilience and coping strategies your family develops are your legacy – a testament to the strength, love, and perseverance that characterizes your shared journey. Through this, we see that navigating life's hurdles is not just about surviving but thriving together as a cohesive, resilient, and loving unit.

Chapter 7:
Celebrating Growth and Achievements as a Family

In this journey of nurturing a healthy, resilient family, pausing to celebrate each other's growth and achievements is not just a joyful detour; it's a vital checkpoint that fuels further progress. Think of it as weaving a tapestry of memories and lessons learned, where each thread represents a milestone or a challenge overcome. This chapter is dedicated to embedding a culture of recognition and positivity within the heart of your family dynamic. It's about turning the spotlight on both the monumental and the seemingly mundane victories, teaching us that every step forward, no matter its size, is a triumph worth acknowledging. Celebrating as a family strengthens bonds, builds self-esteem, and embeds a sense of belonging and achievement in each member. But it's more than just throwing a party. It's about integrating a mindset where every family member feels seen, valued, and motivated to keep growing. Whether it's acing a test, learning to ride a bike, securing a new job, or simply mastering a new healthy recipe—every achievement contributes to the family's collective spirit and momentum. In cultivating a practice of appreciation, you're not only acknowledging past successes; you're laying the groundwork for future endeavors, instilling a perpetual cycle of growth and gratitude. So let's dive into creating and nurturing this culture, ensuring that each family member's efforts and achievements are celebrated, thereby solidifying the foundation for an optimistic, unified, and thriving family unit.

Recognizing Individual and Family Milestones

In the journey of family growth and unity, acknowledging each member's accomplishments and the collective progress of the family is paramount. It's about celebrating the big wins, yes, but also not overlooking the smaller victories that pave the way. Whether it's a child's first step, a teenager's academic success, a parent landing a new job, or the family achieving a goal they set together, every milestone deserves its moment.

Why focus on these milestones, you ask? It's simple. Celebrating these moments fosters a strong sense of belonging and worth within each family member. It sends a powerful message that everyone's personal achievements, no matter the scale, contribute to the family's collective identity and success. Plus, it turns the spotlight on positive aspects of life, encouraging more of the same. It's a nurturing cycle, where recognition and celebration lead to motivation and further achievements.

However, it's not just about throwing a party or handing out rewards. The essence of recognizing milestones lies in the genuine acknowledgment and shared joy among family members. It's in those heartfelt conversations, the proud glances exchanged, and the creation of lasting memories together. By personalizing how you celebrate - be it through a quiet family dinner, a hand-written note of congratulations, or a shared family activity - you ensure the milestone is honored in a meaningful way that reflects your family's values.

Moreover, this practice helps in setting a positive example of how to deal with success and growth. Kids learn to appreciate their achievements and those of others, cultivating an environment of mutual respect and encouragement. They understand that growth is a continuous process and that every step forward, no matter how small, is significant. This mindset paves the way for them to become resilient, confident individuals who recognize the value in their journey and that of others.

Let's not forget that this journey of recognizing milestones is not a solo endeavor. It requires a concerted effort from all family members to actively participate and cherish each other's milestones. The goal is to build up a family culture where growth, in all its forms, is celebrated, and every family member feels seen, valued, and motivated. In doing so, families can weave a stronger tape of unity, appreciation, and collective pride that stands the test of time.

Creating a Culture of Appreciation and Positivity

At the core of every thriving family unit lies the rich soil of appreciation and positivity. Fostering such an environment doesn't come without effort - it requires consistent cultivation, much like tending to a garden. It involves recognizing and celebrating not just the grandiose achievements but also the small victories and efforts. Imagine the boost in confidence your child receives when you acknowledge their attempt to set the table, even if the forks and knives are not perfectly aligned. It's about creating a space where family members feel seen, heard, and valued.

Initiating this culture starts with simple yet impactful actions. Verbal affirmations and expressions of gratitude can light up someone's entire day. Think about the last time someone genuinely thanked you for a meal you prepared or for tidying up the living room. Didn't it make you feel appreciated and more inclined to repeat the gesture? This cycle of positivity, when practiced regularly, can drastically improve the overall mood and emotional well-being of the family. Encouragement should become a daily ritual - a consistent reminder that each family member's contributions to the household are important and appreciated.

Moreover, integrating this appreciative mindset into everyday interactions goes beyond verbal affirmations. It's about actively listening to each other's thoughts, feelings, and experiences without judgment. It means carving out time in our often-hectic schedules to engage in activities that foster family bonding and show that we value each other's presence. Whether it's a family game night, a leisurely walk in the park, or teaming up to tackle household chores, these moments of togetherness are pivotal. They reinforce the message that each family member is an integral part of the team. By embedding a culture of appreciation and positivity within the family dynamics, we lay the foundation for a supportive and nurturing environment where everyone can flourish.

Moving Forward as a Unified, Healthy Family

In embarking on this journey together, we've laid the groundwork for a transformation that reverberates through every aspect of our lives. Navigating the path of health, wellness, and unity as a family isn't just an endeavor; it's a commitment to continual growth, understanding, and love. This closing chapter isn't an end but a beginning—a starting point for families ready to embrace change and foster an environment where every member thrives.

At the heart of our discourse is the unshakeable belief that health is multifaceted, encompassing the physical, mental, and emotional well-being of each family member. The journey we've undertaken together underscores the significance of integrating all aspects of health into our daily lives. It's about finding balance in our meals, joy in our physical activities, peace in our mental practices, and strength in our emotional connections. The path forward is about nurturing these elements in unison, not isolation.

Nutrition, as we've discovered, is a family affair—a collaborative process that values the input and needs of each individual while aiming for the collective good. It's about making balanced meals an adventure that everyone looks forward to, an opportunity to bond over the joys of cooking and the delights of tasting. This collaborative approach extends to managing dietary challenges and embracing diversity in our food choices, ensuring everyone feels seen and heard.

Fitness, too, has emerged as a cornerstone of a vibrant family life. It's more than just routine exercise; it's about creating a culture of movement that fits each person's unique needs and preferences. From playful outdoor activities to structured workouts, the act of moving together strengthens our bodies and our bonds. It's about celebrating each other's successes and encouraging one another during struggles, embodying the notion that we're in this together.

Embracing mindfulness and stress management techniques has taught us the power of being present—both with ourselves and with each other. Implementing these practices within the fabric of family life fosters a sense of calm and resilience, equipping each of us to navigate life's ups and downs with grace. It's about creating a peaceful refuge within our family unit, a safe space where stress is managed collectively, and mindfulness is nurtured as a shared value.

The implementation of routines and structures has offered us a framework within which flexibility and spontaneity can flourish. It's recognized the need for balance—how the predictability of routine can provide a comforting backdrop against which the unexpected joys of life can play out. These rituals, no matter how simple, become the threads that weave the tapestry of our family story, imbuing our days with meaning and connection.

Moreover, mastering the art of communication and navigating difficult conversations have paved the way for deeper understanding and empathy among us. By fostering an environment where emotions are acknowledged and validated, we've created a foundation of trust and openness. It's about embarking on a collective journey towards emotional health, where challenges are met with collective strength and resilience.

Celebrating our growth and achievements has reminded us that every milestone, no matter how small, is a testament to our journey. It's about cultivating a culture of appreciation and positivity, where each person's contributions to our family's growth are recognized and celebrated. This practice of acknowledgment reinforces our commitment to one another and to the journey we're on together.

As we move forward, let us do so with the understanding that our journey is perennial. The landscape will change, challenges will arise, and our needs will evolve. Yet, at the heart of this journey is our unbreakable bond—a commitment to support, nurture, and love one another fiercely and tenderly, in equal measure. This isn't the culmination but the continuation of a voyage we embark on daily, with each step taken together forging our path toward becoming a unified, healthy family.

In closing, let this book not be a final word, but rather a compass guiding you towards a horizon brimming with possibility. As you turn each page of your family's story, remember the strength within your unison and the power of your collective commitment to health and happiness. Here's to moving forward, together, as a unified, healthy family, embracing each moment with courage, love, and an unwavering belief in each other.

Appendix A:
Resources for Continued Family Development

As we come to the close of our journey together in this book, it's important to remember that the path to a healthy, unified, and continuously developing family doesn't end here. In fact, this is just the beginning. To support you on your onward journey, we've gathered a collection of resources that can serve as your compass, guiding you toward sustaining and expanding the gains you've made. Let's dive into these valuable tools.

Recommended Reading and Websites

Knowledge is power, especially when it comes to fostering the health and well-being of your family. In this ever-evolving world, staying informed can help you stay ahead, empowering you with the latest insights and practical advice on family health, nutrition, fitness, mental wellness, and parenting. Here's a carefully curated list of books and websites that can serve as your go-to resource for continued learning and inspiration:

- **The Whole-Brain Child** - An invaluable read that offers revolutionary strategies to nurture your child's developing mind.

- **Nourishing Traditions** - A guide that revisits traditional food preparation and consumption practices, enriching your family's nutritional journey.

- **Parenting From the Inside Out** - This book helps you understand how your own childhood experiences affect your parenting style and how to break the cycle.

- *FamilyEducation.com* - An extensive online resource offering insightful articles and tools for various aspects of parenting and family life.

- *ChooseMyPlate.gov* - A government resource that simplifies nutritional information, helping families make healthier eating choices.

- *PsychologyToday.com - Parenting Section* - Provides thoughtful articles on mental and emotional wellness for parents and children alike.

Local and Online Support Groups for Parents

Beyond the pages of books and websites, sometimes what we truly need is the compassionate understanding that comes from shared experiences. Local and online support groups can provide you with a sense of community and a space to share struggles, victories, and invaluable parenting hacks. Whether you're a new parent feeling a bit overwhelmed, or a seasoned caregiver looking for new ideas, there's a group out there for you. Here's how to find them:

Meetup.com: An extensive platform with groups for just about everything under the sun, including parent support groups. You can find groups in your local area or start your own.

Facebook Groups: With its global reach, you can connect with parents from around the world. From groups focused on mindfulness practices for families to forums discussing the ins and outs of nutrition for kids, there's a community for everyone.

Your local library or community center: Often, these are hubs for parenting workshops and groups. They can also guide you toward additional resources relevant to your family's needs.

Remember, the journey of parenting and family development is unique and full of surprises. It's okay to seek help, continue learning, and most importantly, celebrate every step of progress. These resources are not just tools but stepping stones to building an enduring, loving, and resilient family dynamic. Here's to your family's continuous growth and development—may your path be filled with joy, health, and endless discoveries.

Recommended Reading and Websites

The journey towards a stronger, healthier family doesn't end with the last page of this guide. In fact, it's just beginning. As you continue to explore and grow together, it's invaluable to surround yourselves with resources that inspire, educate, and guide you along this path. Within the realm of recommended reading and websites, there's a wealth of knowledge waiting to be discovered, each providing unique insights into the complexities and joys of family life.

Books offer a deep dive into topics that matter the most to you. Whether it's understanding the nuances of family dynamics, unlocking the secrets to better health and wellness, or finding joy in every moment together, there's a book out there for every situation. From classics that have stood the test of time to contemporary works that tackle modern challenges, these reads can serve as your companions and mentors. They're not just books; they're tools for transformation, capable of igniting conversations and sparking the kind of growth that brings families closer.

Meanwhile, the digital world is brimming with websites dedicated to family development. These platforms are treasure troves of articles, forums, and interactive tools designed to support families in every aspect of their journey. From expert advice on nutrition and fitness to forums where parents can share stories and solutions, these websites offer immediate access to a supportive community and a wealth of information. They're not just about finding quick tips; they're about connecting with others who are on the same path, learning from their experiences, and discovering that, no matter the challenge, you're not alone.

We encourage you to explore these resources with an open heart and mind. Each book you read and every website you visit can offer perspectives that challenge and expand your own. They can provide comfort during tough times and celebrate with you in moments of triumph. However, it's important to remember that the true power of these resources lies not just in their ability to inform but in how you use them to foster communication, understanding, and love within your family.

As you move forward, keep in mind that the goal isn't just to grow as a family but to thrive together, creating a legacy of health, happiness, and unity. Let these recommended readings and websites be your guide, your support, and your inspiration as you continue on this incredible journey. Embrace the learning, the challenges, and the joys ahead, knowing you have the tools and the community to help you through every step.

Local and Online Support Groups for Parents

Embarking on the journey of parenting, much like venturing into uncharted territories, can often feel daunting and isolating. Yet, it's crucial to remember that you're not alone in this journey. Local and online support groups for parents have emerged as vital resources, providing a safe haven for sharing experiences, challenges, and victories. These groups offer more than just advice; they provide a sense of community and understanding that can be incredibly empowering. Whether it's discussing strategies for dealing with picky eaters or finding emotional support during times of family strife, these forums have become indispensable for parents seeking solace and camaraderie.

In the digital age, the accessibility of online support groups allows parents to find communities that resonate deeply with their individual family dynamics and parenting philosophies. From specialized forums focusing on single parenting, special needs advocacy, to general parenting support, there's a treasure trove of wisdom to be discovered online. These platforms enable the sharing of resources, insightful advice, and, perhaps most importantly, the realization that you're part of a larger, global community of parents facing similar trials and triumphs. The beauty of these groups lies in their diversity and inclusivity, ensuring that every parent can find a corner of the internet that feels like home.

On the other hand, local support groups offer the invaluable benefit of face-to-face connection and immediate community engagement. Participating in local parent groups allows for the formation of real-life bonds, offering opportunities for children to grow together and for families to weave their lives into the fabric of their community. These groups often organize meet-ups, workshops, and family-friendly events, fostering a supportive network that thrives on personal interaction. Embracing the support of both local and online groups empowers parents to navigate the complexities of family development with confidence, understanding, and a sense of belonging. In the tapestry of family growth, these groups stitch together patches of wisdom, laughter, and support, illustrating that while parenting is indeed a profound responsibility, it's also a shared experience meant to be nurtured in the company of others.